With Love

to

All My Neighbors

Martha Hernandez

ISBN 979-8-88832-650-3 (paperback)
ISBN 979-8-89345-369-0 (hardcover)
ISBN 979-8-88832-651-0 (digital)

Christian Faith Publishing
832 Park Avenue
Meadville, PA 16335
www.christianfaithpublishing.com

Printed in the United States of America

Acknowledgments

I would like to acknowledge my utmost thanks to my husband, Mike, who always showed a quiet supportive patience, which gave me the peace I needed to pen the thoughts the Lord was giving me. That time was necessary, and he provided it.

Also my son, Mike Jr., I could not have gotten this accomplished without his help. At eighty-five with my eyesight limited and minimal computer skills, it would have been impossible. He had the God-given desire and skills to do this, and he did. No easy task for sure.

To my immediate family for all the support and help whenever and whatever was needed to get the job done.

To Eddie for working on the cover graphics.

God has blessed us with each other for these many years, for which I am so grateful.

Love, Mom.

Introduction

This book is solely for one purpose—to exalt the Lord God Almighty. He has done for me what no other could do. He has redeemed, restored, and brought me to *Himself.* He has taught me what life is truly about—*Him.*

He has given each of us our time on this earth, to see His majesty and splendor, to walk with Him, to wonder at His wonders, to love our brothers and sisters (our neighbors). We are in His image. That is a wonder in itself. Once we understand that, He is so happy, and we will be too.

God has pain when He is rejected by us. When we fall in love, we definitely want to be loved back. He loved us first. He longs for us to love Him back, since He is God and has given us life. He has the answer for all of earth's problems (Romans 3:23). *He,* though *God* of all, paid for each of our sins so we could be restored to *Himself.* Isaiah 53 describes *Jesus* and His *sacrifice* for each and every one of us! Isaiah prophesied this approximately seven hundred years before it happened.

Romans 10:9 says, "That if thou shalt confess with thy mouth the Lord Jesus, and shalt believe in thine heart that God hath raised him from the dead, thou shalt be saved."

Luke 13:3 states, "I tell you, Nay: but, except ye repent, ye shall all likewise perish."

It becomes the *abundant life* (John 10:10). No matter what comes in this life.

This life is *temporal.* After this one, the next is *forever* with Him, and that is what He wanted all along.

This endeavor (my book) is a way to tell a lot of people about the Lord God Jehovah.

What He has done for me, He wants to do for you.

Praise the Lord for all His wonderful works (Luke 8:39).

Story Behind Poem
"The Old and New Martha"

These words came to me after I had been a believer for several years. Looking back over my life, trying to understand myself, God brought me to this conclusion:

When we run from God for whatever reason, real problems come. The worst problems are the ones we cause ourselves. Other people's sins can hurt us, but they cannot destroy us. No, that is done by our own responses and choices. This is what I had to admit and deal with. Every sin we ever commit is done willfully. We always know we shouldn't, but, for whatever reason, we do it. We can't blame anyone else. We do it to get something out of it (and something we like or we will not do it again).

God, in His great love, showed me this truth. As I looked at my life, it was like standing outside of myself and studying my story. It brought me peace, and with compassion, I put the old Martha to rest forever. She is gone, and in her place, the new Martha lives in Christ. My story is good now, and all the praise goes to my Lord.

The Old and New Martha

I knew this one named Martha,
we were together all the way
yet I never understood
her thoughts, her dreams, her ways.

It was impossible you see,
she was always so confused.
her life would make her so perplexed,
so she thought what's the use.

This girl was lonely deep inside,
and yes, was wicked too.
yet it wasn't quite her way,
to evil to be true.

It always made her sad,
when she gave into wrong.
yet to rise above it,
she couldn't do for long.

Her weaknesses would drag her down,
her lack of inner strength.
yet she wanted to do right,
no matter what you think.

She did some things in those years,
that would cause her much regret.
but there was Jesus watching her,
who loved her even yet.

He knew the inner self of her,
He knew what she could be.
so He gently led her,
to the cross of Calvary.

There she was forgiven,
the old Martha surely died.
only to rise brand-new in Him,
the new Martha now am I.

Sometimes now I think of her,
and with peace I understand.
she simply couldn't find her way,
for no one ever can.

There is no life outside of Christ,
I've said all this to say.
I now live complete in Him,
The Truth, The Life, The Way!

Story of "Free"

This song, "Free," came to me, believe it or not, while I was in my car. I loved to drive. Whenever I would get blue, I would jump in my car and go for a ride. Driving was like therapy. It would soothe my nerves. Well, this day, I was struggling with some issues my kids were having. After I got restored to the Lord, I tried my best to catch up. We put them in a Christian school, catch up, catch up is what I wanted to do. *Futile*! Better to live right in the present and believe God for the future.

The kids were messing up some, and I was having a pity party. I used to be really good at that. Now much better (I think). I was thinking how I drove the school bus for their school for seven years. I handed my check back to the secretary almost every time to help pay for their tuition. I had so wanted them to get it. They did, but time had to prove it, and I was impatient. Anyway, as I was driving down a road, these thoughts came. *Why did you do it, Martha? Was it because you just wanted your kids to come out right or was it because you believed in me?* I thought about that really good. I told the Lord these exact words, and I meant them! Lord, no matter what the outcome, I would do it all over again. Lord, I believe in you, and I love You so much!

Before I got back home, He had already given me the first verse of "Free." The rest came a short time later. The tune took longer. I sing it to the girls in my jail ministry and tell them it is my testimony. I tell them God will give them theirs. A life with its tests and "moanies," with God's restoration becomes testimonies.

WITH LOVE TO ALL MY NEIGHBORS 5

FREE

Words and Music
Martha Hernandez
(Job 35:10)
VERSE
G   D7
Am7   D7   G
G   G7   C
G   D7   G C G

1. — Lord, I want to thank you for all you've done for me, and
2. You freed me from the dark-ness of the pri-son I was in; you
3. — In your word you tell me that's the way it had to be; no
4. — Lord, when the storm clouds of prob-lems crowd my life; and

I could nev-er go back to the life that used to be. The
freed me from the bars and cell I had built with my own sin. You
oth-er one was wor-thy to pay the price to set me free. Keep me
things be-gin to hap-pen and I start to ques-tion why. Give my

sin and con-fu-sion, the in-se-cu-ri-ty; These
bled and died on Cal-vary, rose a-gain, my soul to win; Be-
al-ways in re-mem-brance of your cost at Cal-va-ry; That
spir-it strength to soar up to the heights it ought to be; And

things my life was filled with un-til you came and set me free.
cause you're God al-might-y and yet, my clos-est friend.
with your blood you pur-chased me the pow-er to be free.
help me to show oth-ers what it means to be set free.

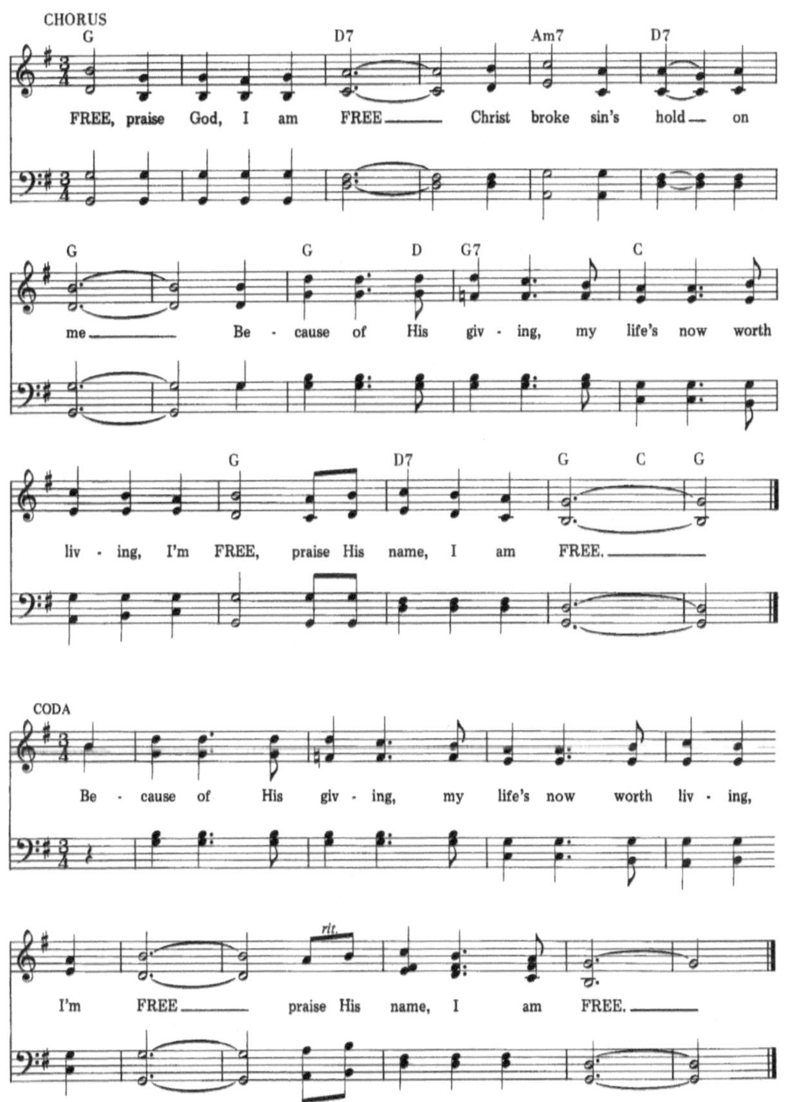

CHORUS
G   D7   Am7   D7
FREE, praise God, I am FREE Christ broke sin's hold on
G   G   D G7   C
me Be - cause of His giv - ing, my life's now worth
G   D7   G C G
liv - ing, I'm FREE, praise His name, I am FREE.
CODA
Be - cause of His giv - ing, my life's now worth liv - ing,
rit.
I'm FREE praise His name, I am FREE.

Food for Thought

Have you ever wondered why (as far as I know) all people worldwide call themselves "I am"? We always introduce ourselves by our first name. For example, I am Martha Hernandez.

The "I am" comes before my name.

The Word of God says in Genesis 1:26, "And God said, let Us make man in Our image, after Our likeness."

Genesis 1:27 says, "So God created man in His Own Image. In the Image of God created he him, male and female created He them."

Exodus 3:14 says, "And God says unto Moses, 'I AM THAT I AM': and He said, 'Thus shalt thou say unto the children of Israel, I AM has sent me unto you.'"

I believe these scriptures answer this question so simply. In fact, the answer speaks for itself.

The God who declares He made us in His image, (by the way, no other god declares this) when speaking of Himself, says, "I AM THAT I AM." I believe the word *that* means He is the real *one*. We are only in *His image*. That is why He has all the answers for life. For this one and the next.

No one can tell God what to do. Since we are in His image. He had to give us freedom to choose Him or not. So it is the way it is. My belief is He is the real I AM. We are only in His image. We certainly need to understand there is only one conclusion—to accept or reject Him.

One Sunday, after church, I drove my grandson home. Before he got out of the car, I reached over and pinched his arm.

As I did, I asked him, "Who is this?"

He looked at me like I was crazy and said, "It's me, Grandma." I pulled down his sun visor and pointed to the mirror and asked who did he see in it. He said, "Me."

I pinched him again (ever so slightly) and said to him, "I thought you said this is you." He got it and smiled. Then I told him, "You see, that's how it is with God. He is the real one. We are just in the mirror, and we should reflect Him."

Story Behind Poem "My Best Friend"

The belief in Bible days, and still holds true, is that people have a tendency to live up to their name.

Most anyone that has read the New Testament has heard about Martha and Mary.

Martha was busy, busy but a worrier. Jesus told her, "Martha, Martha, you are troubled about many things."

Well, I really lived up to the worrier part.

So this is how this poem came to be. We had received an urgent call from my sister, Mary, in Missouri. She needed help, and she needed it *now*. So my husband and I jumped in our truck and took off to help her. Now my husband's nature is the opposite of mine. A big chance taker is more his style, and anyway, who needs to worry? He's got Martha for that. We had a big crew cab truck at that time, and he was in the back seat, stretched out, asleep. Well, true to my nature, I started thinking we hadn't checked out the truck, and it was a one-thousand-mile round trip. I thought of all the things that could go wrong (no cell phones back then). I soon slipped into plain old worrying. Not a happy camper by that time, but 2 Chronicles 16:9a came to mind. I could just imagine two gigantic eyes following me down the highway. About that time, the state line came into view. I remember thinking that those eyes wouldn't stop at the state line. It brought a smile. I started thinking about the promises of God. Then I stopped worrying and just thought on Him. He then put together this poem in my mind.

PS: Our trip was problem free!

My Best Friend

When I begin to worry and my mind starts to fret,
I stop, and start rejoicing for my Lord knows where I'm at.

He sees me every moment, His eyes follow me around.
I'm always in His Presence, His Love for me abounds.

So friend, let's stop our worrying! Let's just get on to the task.
He giveth all provisions, sometimes before we ask.

His promises are faithful, on His Word we can depend.
I'm learning as I'm living.
God Almighty's my best friend.

The Story of My Poem "The Cross"

One of my passions in life was driving. I say was due to my eyesight, I am not able to do as before. It truly was a joy to be behind the wheel. Anyway, my son was moving to California. My aunt and I decided to go with him to see my sister and her family. I loved the thought of the long trip and helping with the driving. There was only one thing that could have stopped me if I had let it. We would have to come back on a plane. I hated the thought of that. I was afraid of flying. Just to think of it would make me nauseous. I was ashamed to admit it, though, because I knew I should trust God and go. I went. The fun of the journey and seeing my loved ones won out. Fun it was.

We were to be there for two weeks. It went pretty fast. One drawback, though, I would count the days before I would take that plane ride. Almost every night, that would happen. I had come across some scripture that comforted me. It was Psalm 91. I prayed and asked God to take my fear and give me peace.

Finally, the day came, I claimed it! We caught the plane! We were surprised at the small number of passengers. We were given pillows and told we could stretch out and sleep if we wanted to. I didn't think I would be able to, but I did.

God had taken my fear, and guess what? When I woke up, I had to use the restroom, and I asked the stewardess how long it would be before we would be in Chicago. She said it would be twenty-five minutes until touchdown. I had slept almost the whole flight. My aunt, who had flown many times, said the landing was the smoothest she had ever experienced. It was perfect. I was so pleased. God had blessed me, and I learned a big lesson about faith.

I saved the best part for last. In Psalm 91:15, 16, actually, the whole chapter is one of my favorites. Verse 15 starts, "He shall call upon Me, and I will answer him, I will be with him in trouble; I will deliver him, and honor him."

Verse 16 states, "With long life will I satisfy him, and show him My salvation."

Now this is the one that just hit me like a ton of bricks.

When I claimed this verse so long ago (at least forty-two years), I thought, *Well, at least I'll get home.* It was just about two years ago I realized a profound truth that hadn't registered before. Since I will be eighty-five in six days, I can say He has also satisfied me with a long life. It brought me to tears when it sank in. Praise the Lord!

No matter how great the day and fun that it would be, I would start thinking about the trip home. I started thinking about Jesus and His trip to earth. I remember asking the Lord if going to the cross before His return home could have spoiled His time on this earth, since it was always before Him. I address this in the poem. Really something to think about.

P.S. Years later, He answered my question. Hebrews 12:2 says, "Looking unto Jesus the author and finisher of our faith; who for the joy that was set before Him endured the cross, despising the shame, and is set down at the right hand of the throne of God."

The Cross

I took a trip to California
I went there in a car.
There was nothing I liked better,
Than going and driving far.

I knew that I would love it
seeing sights and family,
But in my thoughts I wondered,
how my return would be.

You see I knew that at the end,
I'd return home on a plane.
And just the thought of flying,
my joy would start to wane.

Every day brought me closer,
when I would take that dreaded flight.
I'd pray and turn my thoughts to Him,
and He would take my fright.

I started thinking about Jesus.
His trip with man to dwell.
How He did not come for Himself,
but to save our soul from hell.

I thought oh Lord I thank You,
Though You knew how the end would be,
You came with LOVE, lived, died, and AROSE
You did it all for me!

Thirty-three years You faced the Cross,
then bore the Cross alone.
I thank You for Your Sacrifice,
IT BOUGHT MY TICKET HOME.

Story Behind Poem "The Word"

One day, after finishing my devotions, I closed the Bible and just sat there, thinking about it. How much better life was. How much I had learned. Actually, how beautiful truth is! I remember thinking about my life and the change in it.

The profound question was where would I be without it?

I had been told studying it at first would be like taking medicine. You take it because it is good for you. Then it becomes like eating dry cereal. Finally, it becomes like eating peaches and cream. That is a fact. That is how it was when I wrote this poem and still is. I have learned to love it. As you will read in the poem ("The Word"), it can be the same for you.

The Word

Where would I be without you in my life
how could I face each new day
who can know what it may bring
how could I know the right way

You give me such inner peace
when things in my life fall apart
When darkness overwhelms my soul
You speak quietly to my heart

You are the WORDS of life for me
You are the source of stability
You are life's true security
You are the WORDS that have made me free

You never change, forever the same
Words, Spirit, and Life for each day
Revelation proclaims, You are my Lord's Name
You're the Truth, the Life, and the Way!
Revelation 19:13

The Story to the Song "Abundant Life"

This song was written sitting on the back of a motorcycle. I was really learning to trust God and Mike's judgment (still a work in progress but much better). I think we have a tendency to live up to our name. Remember, my name is Martha.

I have met many Marthas, and good worriers they seem to be. Not that they want to be, it seems to go with their name. At least the ones I've met seem to worry a little more than others.

Most sermons I have heard about Martha and Mary (my sister's name is Mary), the story tells that Mary is doing the right thing. Jesus tells Martha she is troubled about many things. I would hear that and think, *But she was doing the things that needed to be done.* Yes, she was, but in a fretting kind of spirit. Nor was she taking time with Jesus first as Mary was. The story goes on to say Jesus loved Martha, her sister, Mary, and their brother, Lazarus (John 11:5). Martha knew His speaking truth in love helped her out too.

In most of the sermons I heard about Martha and Mary, this point was understandably pointed out. One sermon hit a beautiful chord with me. The minister said, and I quote, "One thing about Martha, she knew when she had a problem, and she knew who to take it to!" With a smile, I thought, *Well, Mary, how do you like that?* I wanted to run to the podium and hug that minister.

I also smile about this story, when I think of Mary, my sister, who has now gone to be with the Lord.

Our son, Mike Jr., was attending Cedarville College in Ohio. He needed some medicine, and Mike was going to make a fast trip and take it to him. I was thinking I should go too. The only thing stopping me was worry. My son called, and as I was talking to him,

I mentioned what I was thinking. This is where the story begins. When he was sixteen, he got a job about twenty minutes away by car. He had worked two weeks exactly. He came home from school and needed a way to get to work. Mike Sr. had taken the car to work. It was pouring rain, and no one who might help was answering the phone. He asked, "Mom, what am I going to do? I can't miss!"

I said, "Mike, I don't know. I guess just take Dad's motorcycle."

He looked at me with a surprised look and said, "Mom, it's pouring rain outside."

Jokingly I said, "It will make a man out of you." To my surprise, he rode through the rain, made it to work, and did fine.

Now fast forward two years or so, and back to the phone conversation. I was telling Mike Jr. of my fears and said, "What if it starts raining?"

He, of course, replied promptly, "Oh Mom, it will make a man out of you!"

So I went. Was that the end of the story? Not exactly.

Everything was good until we started back home. The motorcycle broke down on the interstate. Mike Sr. had to hitch a ride to the nearest town to get what he needed to fix the bike. So he left, and I was stuck there with the motorcycle. The cars were whizzing by, and, all of a sudden, a car pulled up. The car looked funny, the guy looked funny. He got out and asked me if I wanted a ride. I said no, thanked him, and mentioned my husband should be returning any second. I could see he lived in his car. I would have been kinder under different circumstances, but it was what it was. Worry kicked in now! He got back into his car and just sat there, watching me.

Well, I had really prayed before we left home, and I told the Lord I would just trust Him and not worry about anything. I'm just about to slip on that one. Torn between trusting and worrying, God showed up, right on time! I saw a couple go by on a motorcycle. They waved as bikers always do, and I waved back. Well, a few minutes later, they pulled up right behind the guy's car. He took off immediately. They told me as they went by, they had noticed my situation looked bad. They decided to come back and check it out. They stayed with me until Mike returned. The bike got fixed, they rode along with us until Indianapolis, and then we headed north. They were like angels on a motorcycle. They were sent by God, and I'm still learning *that is how He works*! Actually, I had started on this song before the trip and was inspired to finish it while on the back of the motorcycle. It was such a joyful time the rest of the way home.

ABUNDANT LIFE

Words & Music
By
MARTHA HERNANDEZ

Abundant Life

Words and Music
MARTHA HERNANDEZ

C
CHORUS
G7
heav - en I serve to - day!
Cal - va - ry," At Cal - va - ry He
heav - en I serve to - day!
Dm/C C G7 Dm/C C
saved me, At Cal - va - ry He for - gave me;
C7/F F
He took the old life where Sa - tan had en - slaved me,
C G7 C
And in its place a - bun - dant life He gave me.
Abundant Life - 2

Perfect Love Casts Out Fear

1 John 4:18–John14:27

Spirit of fear, for many years,
you hung around the closest
And yes I'd let you stay and dwell
You took control the mostest.

It wasn't good for sure I'd say,
You spoiled for me many a day.
Though the sun was shining upon my home
There you'd be, never left me alone

You'd start fretting and fussing
'til the worst I would think
that some bad thing would happen,
and my heart would start to sink

I could have stopped you a long time ago.
There is a TRUTH that makes this so
Having Christ in my heart puts first things first.
Then trusting His Word puts you in reverse.

Real fast it will back you out the door
You cannot torment me anymore.
This is a fact; in God I can trust.
On you spirit of fear He has made the bust.

I'm to love and trust *Him*, and forgive all others
(I can't love Him and yet hate my brother.)
When this is a given in peace I'll be livin'
With this peace my spirit can soar
Fear you're outcast, your power is past.
I will live in the PEACE of my LORD

Food for Thought

Adam lived for 930 years. He had many, many, many years to tell the garden story. He had been influenced by Eve to be disobedient. Though it is tragic, it is somewhat funny. The human tendency to play the blame game still holds true today. Eve blamed the serpent, Adam blamed Eve, and God, with the statement, "It is the woman you gave me." Since man pretty much ruled, his story ruled. It went to many generations. All people spoke the same language until the tower of Babel. Then God dispersed people all over the world and gave them different languages and probably different colors. Though they could not understand different languages to tell stories, all countries knew a story similar to the one of Adam and Eve. Could this be the explanation for man treating woman as he did all over the world? He treated her as a second-rate person, though he needed her to create other persons, his children. He needed her to complete his life and have a family. I am bringing this up to ask, "Doesn't this answer the question that has no logical answer but a biblical one?"

The Bible tells us Adam was rebellious, but Eve was deceived. When mankind knows the Word of God, rebellion and deception disappear.

The Word of God holds every answer to life!

Joy

You can't rob me of my joy
I didn't get it from you
You can't shake it, you can't break it
No matter what you say or do
I received my joy from Jesus Christ
when I was born again
You can't rob me of my joy
for my joy comes from Him
His joy will always be my strength
no matter each day's test
The Holy Spirit lifts me far above
He works so I can rest
The Word forever settled
At the Father's Right Hand sits
The Spirit through His Word
my lowly heart does lift
My state of mind depends
on how I choose to think
When I claim and stand upon His Word
His Joy will be my strength.

Story Behind "Age"

Around the age of fifty, I started to think about age. I had not given it too much thought until then. I didn't want to dwell on it and get caught up in that thinking as so many do. I knew, though, each day was a gift from God.

Time brought many changes and some rough sailing. I prayed about it and asked God to give me His thoughts on it. He did! This poem is the result! It seemed it came to me within minutes. It covers it all and blessed my heart. I hope it blesses yours.

Age

I said to age, "Well, here you are!"
you're here to grow old with me?
I don't remember asking you to,
you're not one I want to see!
I liked you so when I was young,
I thought you were great and would always be fun!
Now here you are with reality,
with aches and pains and wrinkles for me!

Get out of here, get out of my sight, you're
nothing but slowness, trouble, and fright!
Age stood his ground and said, No I won't go,
you've got to stop this resenting me so!
You have got to stop saying you're no friend of mine,
remember it's God who decides your time!
You're forgetting each day is a gift from Him,
I'm living proof you've been blessed my friend!

You've asked Christ into your heart, so don't you complain!
I'm just for earth's time, you've got Heaven to gain!
The day will come we'll go out together, to never meet again!
Almighty God will take you home, to live,
AGELESS, ETERNAL…WITH HIM!

The Glory Side

Living on the Glory Side is something we can do
Living on the Glory Side will always see you through
Each day presents a challenge for this truth to be applied
If you learn to do this well, you will be surprised

Don't be a nipper and don't be a yipper,
which is always the natural to do
Don't be a picker, but do be a flipper
For this is what gets you through

You may be a wonderin' that I'm just a funderin'
But I'm as serious as I can be
Stopping the nip and starting the flip
Is what is the thing that helps me

Small things like the mouth
Can send all things south
Circumstances can also be stoppers
Little mean stuff, can make things be tough
A small skirmish turns into a whopper

Pretend there's a switch in the back of your mind
You can flip when you need, at a moment's time
This switch to good thinking to make your heart sound
Is the same one that brings the Glory Side down

Story Behind "It's a Beautiful Day in the Neighborhood"

One morning, I was having a hard time with my emotions! I was thinking about the loss of a beloved grandson. He was only thirty-one and such a superb young man! I could not understand why! Knowing myself as I did, I knew it could lead to a depressed day and to a downward spiral. I had learned how to think, and I knew I had to put my thinking on the Lord.

I turned to look out of the picture window, and I saw how beautiful the sun was shining. A bird flew pretty close by, and this thought came in my mind, *It is a beautiful day in the neighborhood.* I thought, *Where did that come from?* Right away, I thought of Mr. Rogers. I hadn't watched him very much but knew enough to know that was his trademark saying. That brought a smile to my face. These words came to me that made up this song. I called my family and friends and shared it with them. We were all smiling! If I hadn't flipped my thinking switch, I would have missed it. God honors our efforts to think right and understands it isn't easy. He understands our heart.

That thought brings such a comfort to my heart.
Psalms 103:13-14

It's a Beautiful Day in the Neighborhood

First/Chorus:
It's a beautiful day in the neighborhood!
It's a gift from the Father so let's live it good
Let's show love, compassion, and forgive as He would
cause it's a beautiful day in the neighborhood

Second:
It's a beautiful day, it's a beautiful day
Says the little woodpecker as he's pecking away
Every peck on the wood says um it's good
It's a beautiful day in the neighborhood

Third:
It's a beautiful day, it's a beautiful day
Says the family of beavers as they're gnawing away
every gnaw on the wood says um it's good
It's a beautiful day in the neighborhood

Fourth:
All creation groaneth for that perfect day
Waiting for Jesus in their God-given way
He'll make all things perfect as only He could
When He rules and reigns in our neighborhood

Story Behind "Animated Corpses"

Based on Ephesians 2:4–5

I happened to be working for a trucking firm at the time. As the men came to me to get their work papers processed, it didn't take long to know from the way they (not all) expressed themselves that they cared not one whit for Christ or His Word. I thought about that verse, how without Christ we are dead already, so some of these guys are dead men walking. The thought came to me that they were like animated corpses. Animated but not really alive. To me, the thought kind of brought a sadness, for they were hardworking men that did important work.

I have to say here, there were also drivers that were brothers in Christ, and they had a different outlook on things, and it showed. They had life in Christ. I started watching people in general, also thinking how my own life had been (before Jesus). The Lord impressed me with these thoughts, and it became this poem.

Animated Corpses

You are an animated corpse, if your heart is without Christ
You walk around with chains on, bound up in your own vice.
You move, and do, you think you're cool but left with an empty ring
You play the fool, by the enemies' rules and all you see is bling.

Your soul's enemy is satan, he studies you so well,
What he really wants for you, make sure he'll never tell.
He knows all your weaknesses, without Christ you're on your own.
Tells you, your life is yours. You can make the choice alone.

He'll chew you up and spit you out while all the time it's fun.
And you will be oblivious to all the harm he's done…
Convinced this life is you, you, you. What you want is what you do.
Fill your mind with make-believe, that's
satan's plan, and you're deceived.

You go thinking you've got it made. You end up just being his slave.
You have chains on you can't see, living for him, you'll never be free.
You know friend that in the end, the Bible clearly tells.
His sole goal is to keep your soul and take you straight to hell.

The Answer to Animated Corpses

There are two sides to this story,
the story of our soul.
This side is of GLORY,
when we give God control.
He designed each one of us,
He made us in His image.
To keep us free, gave you and me,
the choice, to decide our finish.

Adam and Eve, ate of the fruit,
Self-rule was their choice that day.
Now we are born, (we can't refute),
with the desire to disobey.
When we do, God calls it sin,
the penalty is death.
Self-love rules, not love for Him,
though He loves us even yet.

He sent His Son, to pay for our sin.
His love compelled it so.
Jesus, came, our soul to win,
He died and then arose.
He paid sin's debt, for you and me,
so we have no excuse.
The Bible plainly tells us
it is all in how we choose.

Choose life, choose Him, be born again
He will set you free.
To live with Him, your greatest FRIEND
for now and eternity.
He's the giver of LIFE
the TRUTH, THE LIFE, THE WAY,
The Bible's great love story.
It is His goal to win your soul,
then, give you a home, in His GLORY

Story of "Bring Back the Glory"

My daughter Amber and I were talking about Christmas. It was, as always, a beautiful time for all of us. I remarked about how there weren't many manger scenes in the stores. It was all santa. We were saying how sad it was. The whole celebration was about Jesus's birthday. It had sure gotten lost. We both agreed, if it made us sad, what did the Lord think about it? How would we feel if it was our birthday and everybody else got a gift or all the attention, and we got hardly noticed. I really got serious and wondered how God felt about it and would He share His thoughts on it with me? I asked Him to in a prayer. Well, that night (at about 3:00 a.m.), I woke up just as though someone had tapped me. I just lay there, wide awake, looking up at the ceiling. I wondered if I should just get up. All of a sudden, a thought came to me:

It was, *Lord, looking through the eyes of You, what did santa ever do?* That is the way He starts my poems.

I sat up. I knew God was giving me His thoughts. A poem.

He did! This beautiful poem!

I am telling you these are His thoughts about santa claus, one of the biggest fallacies that has ever been told. I know, in many ways, it is unintended. It sounds so nice, so cute, harmless, and gives kids something to enjoy.

I want to say this. When I was a young mother, not thinking about Jesus, certainly not living for Him, we had a neighbor who had a santa claus suit and wore it over on Christmas Eve. I just did it for fun. We hadn't taught our kids to believe in santa. They didn't, so I thought it was okay. We told them the gifts were from us and family. They knew we would buy them the special things they wanted (within reason) for their birthday and Christmas. Kids are mostly into the gift, not how it came. Teaching them the truth will help them to be grateful as they grow to adulthood, when they have to work and pay for things!

I had Christmas decorations also with both santa and Jesus. Never thought too much about it then. When I started walking with the Lord, I began to see the error in my thinking. I saw how so much was put on santa and the lie behind it. It is a lie told to little ones who could have a real Lord, who made the moon and stars, and, yes, them as well. There are no reindeers pulling santa all over the world.

There *is the one* who made the spinning ball we live on, who wants to be our best friend *forever*. For all time, hanging out together with their *best friend*, Jesus, who in heaven, someday, just maybe will show them how to send a shooting star across the sky. So much to look forward to and never have to worry again or be sad, have pain, every animal a friend, visit the stars, maybe make one, who knows? All good, good, good! Remember, they are taught there is a santa claus up in the heavens with his reindeer they can't see. They believe in that! Why make up a fake story when there is Jesus? Talking about reindeer flying, oh, someday, my friend, you can fly, and you won't need reindeer. They will only keep up with you when you slow down and let them (if reindeers are in heaven).

Tell the little children that story, so when you teach them to tell you the truth, you won't be sorry you lied to them first. Whoever is reading this poem, please know I love you and count you as a friend I have never met. This is what my studying has brought me to think! I am sharing what God has given me.

I do want to tell you what happened. What the Lord did. I submitted that poem into a church contest. I didn't win, but I got an honorable mention. The girl that won deserved the win. She acted hers out and did a superb job. Anyway, the results were posted in the paper. A short time later, I got a call. They asked me if I would come and teach poetry to grade school kids at Franklin School in East Chicago, Indiana. I was shocked. I almost said no. I couldn't teach what I hadn't learned. Yet I felt God was behind it, so I decided to go (scared, but I went). They did say I wasn't to mention God, if possible. They didn't say it emphatically, so I thought, *We'll see.* Since I knew this was all His doing, I went and my sister, Mary, went along to be my moral support. She was a help for sure. God showed up, and He showed off!

It was an experience which I address in the story, the "Life Poem." God just took over.

Bring Back the Glory

Lord, looking through the eyes of You,
what did santa ever do?
Just because a simple man,
once gave gifts in a foreign land.
Not knowing his story would be told,
taking away from the one of old.

Oh, they say it's all in fun,
lighten up there's no harm done.
Christmas is for kids you see,
you take it far too seriously!
Yet in Your Word I plainly read,
let the children come to Me.

In this land year after year,
this is so much of what I hear.
Santa knows when you are glad,
and santa knows when you are bad.
Oh Lord what have we done,
santa has replaced Your Son!

Lord, looking through the eyes of You,
what did santa ever do?
Could he ever take my shame,
could he ever take my blame?
Could he ever pay the price,
and become my sacrifice?

Could he give new life to me,
a life for all eternity?
No Lord looking through Your eyes of Truth,
let my heart be stayed on You!
No one else can share Your Story,
You alone must have the Glory.

Food for Thought

Have you ever seen a picture of Jesus by an artist? He looks perfectly handsome! Have you ever seen a picture of satan by an artist? Doesn't he look horrid and ugly? Now think, why is that? Isn't it funny? The Bible tells the opposite of them. In Isaiah 53:2, about Jesus. In Ezekiel 28:11–19, about satan.

Man draws from the results he sees in a life coming from a relationship of the one he serves. A born-again Christian could never draw Jesus anything but beautiful because He makes a life beautiful. On the other hand, satan seeks to steal, kill, and destroy all that's made in the image of God.

John 10:10 sums it up!

Story behind the poem "Life Story" (Psalm 139)

This is based on the whole chapter of Psalm 139.

You will need to look this up and read it for yourself.

I had been asked to teach poetry to children of middle-school age at a public school. This all came about due to the fact I had submitted a poem in a contest, and although I did not win first place, it received enough attention to get my name mentioned in the paper.

The event was church sponsored, yet I was asked not to mention God in my presentation. I wasn't too happy with this. The sponsors weren't either, but this is what we had to work with because it was a public school. I hesitated at first, but I knew God had given me the poem for a purpose, and He alone could show me what it was. So I had to do it. I will say this: my Lord showed up and took over.

He gave me the wisdom I needed for the moment, and it was fantastic. My sister, Mary, went with me to be moral support, and she could attest to this. I got to express many things the kids could relate to. I was pretty good at drawing, so I drew a clown and emphasized that I could never draw it exactly the same again. There would be variation (ever so slight maybe), but, nevertheless, it would be there. For that reason, each drawing would be special (to me for sure because it was mine). I would always recognize my drawing and would know it anywhere. I then brought out how each one of us is special and unique. I went on to say that we are all designed and that our *Designer* knows us like so. I iterated on the fact that if I heard one talking negatively about my drawing, I would not like it, and they wouldn't like it either. They agreed with that as they were trying to draw a clown like mine.

I then brought out why making fun of someone's looks or anything about them (which they had no control over) is really an insult to the *One* who designed them. He takes it personally! It was His drawing, and He loved it. They understood. I told them there is a special purpose for them being here and to shoot for the stars, and even if they fell back on the moon, they were still on high ground. They were sitting cross-legged in front of me and were putting it on paper. God was so much in it that I must interject this here.

At the beginning, there were two teachers, a librarian, and one vice principal, standing in the back, (we were in the library). They were casually listening, but as time went on, they gravitated toward the front and were listening intently. At the end, I got bold enough to ask the kids if they would sign their names on a paper, and that way I could remember them and pray for them. Guess what? The vice principal asked if she could sign it too. She also remarked to my sister that the presentation should be on video and shown to all the schools.

I must tell you, when they showed me their pictures they had drawn that day, I was so touched, it brought tears to my eyes. That God would use me to get His very important facts expressed to them in such a unique way is something I will never forget. I thought about my own life as a child. When I was their age, I did not know that I would have a gift from Him of poetry. I know that He has gifts for them too. Only He knows what they will be. I received my gift after I was born again. I think He wanted my poems to be about Him, and most of them are. All of our gifts are from Him and for His Glory. After all, we are only made for His good pleasure. When we realize this and really want to please Him, we get pretty pleased ourselves. That time with those kids was wonderful, I'd even say glorious! One of those special times of mine on this planet. This is the poem God gave me to present there.

Life Story

You are the author of your story
being written every day.
And you decide just how it will read
By what you do and say.

Your choices are like words
that you must pick and choose.
Everything you say and do
will help you win or lose.

So let the words you speak be good
the bad words just don't say.
Do the things most right to do
and you'll be on your way.

Listen to your teachers
obey your parents too.
And speak into each day you live
the story that makes up YOU.

Remember you are special
whom no one else can be.
Go write your life story beautifully
for everyone to read!

Mothers

Heavenly Father, help me I pray,
to pen Your thoughts about Mother's today
I have mine, they are lovely and sweet,
but from heaven's view, so incomplete.

You are the One who made the plan,
that would bring Salvation to fallen man.
You knew the precise day that would come,
a young Jewish woman would bear Your Son.

She would have the heart to do Your Will
so her part in it would be fulfilled.
She trusted You for the Miracle to come
and said, according to Thy Will, let It be done.

She had no knowledge of what lay ahead,
She simply trusted what the angel said.
Such a beautiful example for us today
to trust You the giver of life, to lead the way.
The virgin Mary, though not divine, had
a mother's heart for all time.

So to all women whatever our role,
let us purpose to follow not in part but the whole.
The Wonderful Word which is God's True Love Story
Praising the Lord, giving God all the Glory.

Mountain Climbing—Story Behind the Poem "Two Ladies of Grace"

I remember thinking one day, the Christian life is like mountain climbing. I was convinced of it. I went to the public library close to our house. They didn't have any books on mountain climbing. I then drove to a big library in the next town, determined to prove to myself an exciting fact. I did!

I checked it out and kept it for a few days. Sure enough, the analogies were in it. So interesting and true.

One of the biggest factors I read was this: most of the falls are not climbing the mountain but going down the mountain. It seems, once one reaches the top, they get overconfident and careless. They do not dig into the rock, and then falls happen.

Proverbs 16:18 states, "Pride goes before destruction, a haughty spirit before a fall."

Two Ladies of Grace

Wanda V. and Me

Two ladies of GRACE sat down for a chat,
they talked about this, they talked about that.
One said, you know dear, that most of the time,
this Christian life is like a mountain climb.

The other said, yes my sister it's true,
looking at it from a heavenly view.
Yes, yes, I can see, the analogy's there,
to climb any mountain, you have to take care.

We know we must always, start out with a plan,
to study, to read, and learn all that we can.
Be rightly equipped, work our plan, with our skills,
and don't forget dear, you have to have will.

Tis true for sure, it's part of the climb,
we know it's just inches, we cover sometimes.
In this walk with the Lord, the climb is the same,
one step-up at a time and all in HIS NAME.

The provision is there, though the storms make it dim,
yet HE gives us HIS WILL, for we're climbing in HIM.
So we just keep climbing, though others might mock,
we smile for we know we've dug into the ROCK!

The ROCK is CHRIST JESUS, our leader THE SPIRIT,
HE calls to climb higher, in our hearts we can hear it!
Then someday my dear when this climbing is o'er,
We'll sit and we'll chat on that Heavenly shore.

Blessing

Lord, bless this house
with Your wonderful love
That only comes from Heaven above
That teaches us how to live and to love.

Father, bless this couple in their endeavors
to keep their vow so it won't be severed
Help them desire the answers You give
For all life's problems and how to live.

Bless them with Your thinking
so they will know how
to keep their promise
when they made that vow.

To love each other for better or worse
in sickness, in health, until the hearse
The vow they took to make a home
The vow they made before Your throne.

Lord, bless this couple
that they might have
Your wisdom that's needed
to be Mom and Dad.

Bless them with Yourself, so their children will know
That You are real from the love that they show
Help them remember their kids are on loan
And to be Godly examples to them in their home.

Bless them to know, it's about You not them
You are their Reality, Life, Way, yet their closest friend
Yes, in You Lord, is their only hope
That when You give Your blessing it can't be revoked!

The Story Behind the Poem and Song "A Prayer that Was Answered"

I was on a camping trip when I had just found out my wonderful daughter was pregnant.

It wasn't in my plans. I had a different dream for her.

I went for a walk and started talking to the Lord as I had learned to do. By the end of my walk, He had given me a song. I never had it published, so it doesn't have any music notes in print. It exists only in my head. After more than forty-two years, I can still sing this song. PS: The dream came true not just for my grandson but for all seventeen of my grandchildren. God is good!

A Prayer that Was Answered
(Poem/Unpublished Song)

I'll dream a dream again

I'll give that dream to Him

That little soul to win

To grow and live for Him

My song shall ever be

Thanks Lord for loving me

My heart will always sing

Thanks Lord for everything!

The Wonder of Love

You have been given a gift from God on loan

To love and enjoy and live in your home

A one of a kind that is made in His Image

Such a wonder of wonders from start to finish!

He sees and knows each detail ahead

So get smart from the start so you can be led

To train and to live so your child will know

God is real, by the life and love to others you show!

Matthew 7:12, Luke 6:31

Lord, You Say

Be ye kind to one another
Lord, do you mean really any other?
You could have made them neater, so they would treat me sweeter

Lord, when You say another, does that seriously mean my brother?
You have got to be kidding, he wants me to do his bidding

Am I my brother's keeper? This just gets deeper and deeper
He's the one who acts like Cain, can't You see I'm not to blame?

Lord, my heart is kind of showing, and I see where this is going
You want me to be like You, no matter what others say or do

So take my heart, You keep it clean, because
on my own, I can be mean
You even love me when I sin, You forgive
me again, again, and again!

Lord, help me to show Your Word to be true,
to show others what You would do
use Your Word as my greatest tool and live
my life by Your Golden Rule!

Matthew 7:12, Ephesians 4:32

Don't Say

You don't have to say everything you're thinking
So be wise, be quiet, and eyes won't be blinking
By your words you're justified, by your words condemned
Keep your mouth shut and you might win or keep a friend.

Every word we say will have some bearing
It will be backed up by the face we are wearing
Take the time, ask the Spirit to impute The Word
Be quiet so His still small voice can be heard.

In your mind, stop, and real slow count to ten
wait, watch, and see, how each battle you win
Wait on the Lord for the battle's His, He will win it
And your victory will be sweet, for His Glory is in it.

Story Behind the "Moving Ball" Poem

My grandson Mark had a school project and asked me if I would write him a poem. He could write it or have someone else write it, but it had to be original. His choice was about sports because he loved sports, especially baseball. I began to think about a ball. I love to analogize, so I used that thinking. I thought how we all live on a spinning ball (the earth) that *only God* can control. Man, who is made *in His image*, loves to control a ball, and when he gets good at it, he gets really noticed, *big time*!

I wrote the poem. Mark liked it, the teacher liked it, and so did I. *I love you, Mark (14). See you later.*

Moving Ball

Can anybody tell me, can anyone explain,
why the whole world over, all kids act the same?
The first time that we see it, we seem to look in awe,
this thing that draws us, is called the moving ball.
It comes in all shapes and colors,
and played with many ways,
and somehow hangs around us
to help us spend our days.

Though many go on to other things,
there are those who stay,
and live their lives to chase it,
in many different ways.

I'd guess you'd say it's in our soul,
this moving ball to master.
To always keep it in control,
and prove that we are faster.

Though now and then it shows us,
that it will have its way.
Tis then the game we lose and leave,
to play another day.

One thing's clear year after year,
there's a story for us all.
We're all different, yet the same.
when it comes to the moving ball

The reason it affects us all?
We all live our lives on a MOVING BALL.

It was made, it's controlled, if only we'll hear it

By THE FATHER, THE SON, AND THE HOLY SPIRIT.

Food for Thought

It has been preached that in Genesis 2:17, it says, "In the day that you eat from it (the tree of the knowledge of good and evil) you shall surely die." That God meant spiritual death.

God showed me many years ago as I was reading 2 Peter 3:8, that one day is with the Lord as a thousand years. In Genesis 5:5, it says, "Adam lived 930 years."

So when God said, "In that day you will surely die," Adam actually physically died, according to God's timetable.

Just something to chew on!

The Meaning of Christmas

The meaning of Christmas spreads joy all around
The beauty of Christmas, none like it is found

For the glory of Heaven, was sent to this earth
The Christ Child Immanuel, God's Glory on earth

The gift of the Father, to all who believe
The Christ Child Immanuel, to all who receive

Jesus the Christ Child, to pay for my sin
God's gift freely given, a new life in Him

New life never-ending, with angels I'll sing
The birth of my Savior, Christ Jesus, the King.

The Story Behind "The Valley"

One night, while sitting, contemplating what two friends of mine were going through, these thoughts came to me.

Their circumstances were very sad. John, the husband, was very ill and not expected to live through the night. His wife, Edie, was there beside him. I began to think how this time comes for all. No one can prevent the final appointed time, which we all have (Hebrews 9:27–28). When it is your loved one, you are completely helpless. Though you would give your life so the one you love could live, it simply cannot be done. There you are with a broken heart and totally helpless to intervene. It is the worst situation to be in. But there it is.

I knew this couple both loved the Lord and had accepted salvation's plan! They had asked the Lord to save them, and He had. I can write this statement with confidence because Jesus says in His Word, whoever cometh to Him, He will, in no way, cast out (John 6:37). That verse alone brought them comfort and me too! This poem God gave me that night, expresses the beauty, the grace, and hope for all of us who have repented and asked Jesus to be our Lord and Savior. He gives us eternal life to live with Him forever! As it says in Psalm 23:4, "Yea, though I walk through the valley of the shadow of death, I shall fear no evil." Some interjection here as to what that means.

A minister was asked this question by his young son, "Dad, what does it mean in Psalm 23 about the shadow of death?"

Trying to think how to explain it simply, he was kind of at a loss. They were in the car, and a semitruck was crossing in front of them, and the sun had cast a big shadow on it. Then, happily, he asked the boy this simple question, "Son, which would you rather be hit by, the truck or by its shadow?"

The boy got it and smiled.

As we can do when we as believers think about death. This truth is for believers only. Death is only a *shadow*! *Oh happy day*! Praise God!

P.S. John lived for three more years after life support was removed!

The Valley

I walked the valley with you, as far as I could go.
The journey ahead was only for you and the Lord to know.
When the time came, I felt my heart just break
Jesus reminded me right then He makes no mistakes.

He had you covered, He would walk you through.
Death was a shadow, there was nothing it could do.
He had taken care of that upon a wooden cross.
He'd won the victory over death, our enemy had lost.

From that point I knew, that we would be apart.
Jesus alone, could mend my broken heart.
There also I knew, a different valley I would walk.
It would be without you, no more seeing, no more talk.

Our life together seemed to race before my mind.
You've gone on before me, and I've been left behind.
I choose to remember, the TRUTH we learned together.
For all of our life's journey, He will leave us never!

The Holy Spirit has lived in us, and He can never die.
So after the last valley, off with Him we fly.
To Heaven and mansions, Jesus made for you and me.
Because of Him, we'll meet again to live eternally.

The Garden Story

In the beginning, God made Adam and Eve. This is where it all began for each of us. They had it perfect, so much to enjoy. They had God walking, and talking, sharing with them in such a beautiful relationship. He had made all creation for them. He had given them dominion over it.

This beautiful garden was made especially for them. There was *just* one command given. They were not to eat of the tree of knowledge of good and evil, but they did.

We think, shame on them, of all things, what was so hard about that? Keep thinking. They did not have a book they could read to warn them, to learn from someone else's mistake. They didn't know anything but good. Who shows up? The enemy of their soul. Now he comes to them, looking beautiful like everything around them looked. He tells them (ever so sweetly, I'm sure) that God is keeping them from knowing good and evil. Notice the lie, they already had it good (as good as good can be). No, he wanted them to know evil, and he knew that evil would get them thrown out of the garden, just like he was thrown out of heaven. You see, he had rebelled against God when he was the top angel of music there (isn't that interesting?). He was so beautiful, and pride got the best of him. He wanted to be equal with God. He said, "*I will,*" and soon, he was not (in heaven that is).

Think, though. He was a created being like Adam and Eve. He was not created in the image of God. They were. He hated God, and he hated the two made in His image (that has never changed). He hates each of us for the same reason. He wants to destroy, maim, and kill us. Here is the catch. When Adam and Eve chose to disobey, that sin nature was passed to all human descendants. We are born with a will to disobey. We don't want rules or boundaries (even though they are good for us).

Keep thinking. Keep it simple. Watch a little child just learning to walk. That toddler is walking toward something. You say no, no, and watch them run to it. They don't understand, and they can't yet, but you and I can. We all have this innate thinking, my life is mine, my body is mine, what I want is what I should have, come whatever. The "I" rules in each of us. We have to be taught good behavior, not so with bad. It is our nature to be self-conscious and self-centered and to self-rule and self-destruct. Think about this—where did this thinking come from? We had nothing to do with us being us. We pop into this world. Everything is already decided for us. Our gender, our color, our parents, personality, and talents. Now here I will share my personal thinking. The first time I learned about death, I was shocked such a thing could happen. I said, "Well, I'm not going to die."

I was then told, "Oh yes, you will. Everything has to die." I still said, "*Not* me." I just got an all-knowing smile. As time went by, I remember coming to this, thinking, *I have to die?* How unfair is that? I didn't ask to come here in the first place. I didn't have any say in any of it, and I have to die to get out of here? How can that be? Doesn't that prove that there has to be a purpose for you and me being here? There is, and God has given His Word on it.

Now back to the garden. Each one of us is born into a garden, so to speak (now comes the thinking part again). Let me state here that I love to analogize. Okay, this is it. We all disobey, and we have to be taught right. We have the choice, from the beginning, to obey or not. Okay, as children, we are kind of off the hook because God knows each of us and only He knows where we are in our thinking and understanding. Approximately around twelve, we really become accountable for our thinking and choices (give or take a year or so. Only God knows each person).

Remember the garden story. Fast forward, same scenario, different time, different people, watch how the enemy of all souls comes with his goodies. He suggests, ever so nicely, that we are missing out on something really good. Drugs, smoking, drinking, and sex are usually the ones he holds out first. With the promise that you will enjoy it, you don't know what you have been missing. Sound familiar?

Yes—ah, now this is a fact of life. Every time we disobeyed, we knew in our heart (and mind) we shouldn't do it. Something in us wanted to (sin nature).

Now back to our problem. Notice if you don't get enjoyment from disobedience, you likely won't do it again (if you like it, you will do it again, thinking, just one more time, then again and again—until it has you). It will be pleasure for a season—the Word of God says this. Think now of the reality. Seasons change, and what was done for pleasure now becomes control, and *you* don't have it. It controls you and exacts a payment. What once was your choice has rendered you controlled as God has warned us in His Word. No longer is it good because it does not last! You have to work to get that good feeling back! Over and over, and each time you do it, you are caught more in its trap. Notice the word *trap*—even the word brings a bad taste in your mouth, doesn't it? That is just what our enemy wanted. We, who are made in the image of our Creator, our God, trapped and helpless to get ourselves free. Make no mistake, the trapped will die in this trap. The trapper has nothing in his DNA of compassion, love, and mercy. That isn't the end. An eternal trap awaits, the name of it is hell, with no way out forever. There is only One who can render the trapper powerless, release the trapped, and set them free (and free indeed). Make no mistake, God is Holy and Just. Sin must be paid for. He has decreed this so. Praise God, for He is a God of love, and even in judgment, He loves mercy. He sent His Son who was sinless.

His body was given for the sacrifice. With His Blood, paid for all of our sin. He sets us free to have control of ourselves through Him and His Word, and the power to obey and cancel out that old sin nature, which only wants us defeated and destroyed.

Here then is reality, God tells us in His Word that we each are created by Him for His good pleasure, not ours. Think about this now. Since we didn't make ourselves (nor anything about us), it does make sense. We have a choice to make. It continues on in every moment we live, until He calls us out. Again, His Word says we all have an appointed time to die. Now between the appointed time to come here and the appointed to leave, we are free to decide our choices. His Word always tells us how much He loves you and me. So much He gave His Son to pay for all of our sin, so we could be reconciled back to Him. If we accept His provision through His Son, we can be restored to our garden. It is called born again (John 3:16)!

Our spirit is united with His Spirit (the Holy Spirit as He is known). From that moment, we are brand-new in Him, like a baby. We can grow up in Him through His Word. We have a relationship with Him, just like Adam and Eve had in the beginning. Remember how they walked with Him and shared with Him? We won't have it perfect. We still live in this sin-cursed world. We will have that old nature trying to raise its ugly head and defeat us. The difference is now we have His Spirit, His Word, and His promises. One thing that has not and will not change until we are out of here is our choice to decide and choose to stay safe and secure inside the boundaries that He has made for our good. This is told to us in *His Word*.

Once we have accepted Jesus and His Blood as the payment for our sin, we are sealed by the Holy Spirit, until the day of redemption. We are a child of the *Most High God! His good* is *good*. We are rescued, redeemed, and restored. The father of all lies is still walking around, trying and lying to get us thinking we know best. Let us put that to rest. Remember our testimony and the price He paid to give us one. Also, when we miss the mark (violate His Word), it is called sin (1 John 1:9). Go sit on the bench, so to speak, like all the sports heroes do when they miss at their mark. Then repent, claim His Blood and forgiveness, and go shoot at the mark again. God has declared us saints (in practical speaking).

The Holy Spirit wrote the Word, and He lives in us. When we violate the Word, He will grieve, and we get depressed. When we are responding according to the Word, He gets happy, and we can't stay depressed (no matter the circumstance). We will all have sadness due to death and tragic happenings in this life. Even Jesus wept. We will too. And we should. Having depression is beyond that. God is the God of *all* comfort. Seeing the problem through His point of view will cause the Holy Spirit to raise you up spiritually, to keep the joy and strength that only Jesus can give. This only has to be done in the day you are in.

Yesterday is gone (covered by His Blood). Tomorrow is in His hands. You only have the present day you are in. Notice the word *present*; it is a gift from the Father. That is why it is called a present.

Keep it current with John 1:9!

The Wheelbarrow

It was beginning to look a lot like Christmas. We had thirty-six gifts to purchase for our thirty six great-grandchildren. It was always a challenge because what we spent on one, we wanted to spend on all.

Well, this one day, I went in a big outlet store, looking for a simple item I needed. While looking, I spied on a pretty glass wheelbarrow. It stood out, just the right size to put on a dresser or shelf. It could hold trinkets, pretties, important items, rings, or such things.

All of the kids could benefit from it. It was pretty and sturdy. Also, it was such a great sale. I could buy thirty-six easy, and I did. I actually purchased forty-six, just in case we needed more in the future.

I had always liked wheelbarrows. Whenever I helped with yard work, I wanted to have one handy. There was only one drawback—a flat tire. Once fixed, it would be so helpful. I took the wheelbarrows and filled them with candy. Each one received a reading on the what and why of their gifts. It would last for a long time and do its job if taken care of, just like the real one does.

I was one happy great-grandma that year!

I started wondering about the wheelbarrow and when it was invented. I thought it was first made approximately a hundred years ago. Was I wrong! It was invented by a man in China around two thousand years ago. It was considered so valuable, it helped to win a war! They wanted to keep it a secret from their enemy. It can carry a load that is impossible for a man to carry alone! That is what it did in the war. It carried many supplies and even brought injured men back to safety. It was a great tool! One, that to this day is a help in carrying heavier loads than we can ever handle alone. I had learned that and always wanted to have one handy. Work and the wheelbarrow go together.

God tells us in Romans 8:28 that "all things work together for good to those who love God and are the called according to His purpose." Well, He also says in His Word, "He neither slumbers nor sleeps!" God is not only a God of love but also a God of work. We are made in His image, so of course we are to work too. Notice He says He will work all things out for our good to those who love Him! He so wants us to love Him! Since He created us, He knows what is best. He wants to be number one because He has the answers for life!

God also wants us to plan our work and work our plan. That is what He did! He had a plan, and it was worked out by Jesus. Though Jesus, God's only Son owned it all, He came to earth and was born in a stable. A lowly manger was His bed. Why wasn't He born to riches and raised in a palace? God wanted us to know that it isn't what you have but who you are that counts! Always remember that! It is okay to have nice things as long as they don't have you. Jesus lived on earth without riches. He was on a mission to live an obedient life to the Father, to help, heal, and pay for our sins because no one else could. He truly worked out the plan of salvation on a daily basis during His time on earth. He lived a temporary life on earth, knowing at the end of thirty-three years, He would be hung on a cross to pay for man's sin! There was no other way! God the Father had declared that the wages of sin is death. Man living for himself, had no thought of His Creator, God. All had sinned. He declared that without the shedding of blood, there is no remission of sin. Only Jesus had lived without sin, and only His Blood could pay for sin.

Man lives a temporary life. Jesus did too. Only Jesus lived His for us, so we could have a permanent life with Him forever in His *eternal home in heaven.* You see, man's sin causes a heavier burden that is more than he can carry. Because of love, Jesus bore that on the cross and carried it away! The Bible says that as far as the east is from the west, so far has He removed our transgression, never to be remembered against us again!

What a work done for all of us!

We only have to believe that God raised Jesus from the dead on the third day.

Ask Jesus to forgive us our sins, come into our hearts, and be Lord and Savior from then on, with an eternal home for each of His children.

See, He is working on our behalf! He rewards His children. He asks us to work for Him in our temporary life on earth. He then gives us a permanent life with Him forever and ever. There will be no more dying, pain, tears, sickness, and no sadness. It is called Heaven!

God loved us first. He longs to be loved by us, but He will not force us to love Him. We all want to be loved because we are made in His image. Never forget. We cannot see Him, and He knows that. He sees all and knows all! When you honor your Heavenly Father, and your life makes Him look good, He will make you look good, and you will have honor. He will work that out for your good too!

Plan your work and work your plan. God did just that.

I put some candy in the wheelbarrow to represent this.

When we get paid for our work or when we get a reward because of hard work, when the project we've worked hard to get finished is looking good, it is a sweet feeling, and even that is a reward in itself. In heaven, there will be rewards and many crowns given to each one that has worked for Him. Remember, He sees all, and nothing goes unnoticed! He is a rewarder to those who diligently seek Him. He owns it all, so look up with a smile on your face, love in your heart for Him first, and He will work all things out for your good and His purpose!

So go to work for Him. Do your part. He will do His!

Christmas Reading

Lord, I pause to remember, your life on this earth.
The Holy plan that You lived out, to give us second birth.
The angel told Your mother Mary, and told Joseph too,
with God she had found favor, she would give birth to You.
The cumbersome ride for Your mother, to pay tax in Bethlehem.
Angelic hosts proclaimed to the shepherds in that distant land,
they would find the babe in a manger,
where Your wondrous life began.
Wise men followed the star to see You, God's glorious Gift to man.

When Herod tried to kill You, the angel with Joseph met,
told him to take Your mother and You to Egypt until Herod's death.
Thus, would be fulfilled the Scripture, Hosea 11:1,
out of Egypt, I have called my Son.
After Herod's death an angel spoke to Joseph in two dreams.
He was to take You to Israel, then Nazareth.
You would be called a Nazarene.

In the temple as a youth, You with the scholars sat.
Your knowledge of the Scriptures made them marvel,
How You could know all that.
You spoke with such authority, it seemed they should tell
That sitting in their midst truly was Emmanuel.
How Your parents panicked when You they couldn't find.
For it was in Jerusalem You had stayed behind.

And You told them, even then You knew,
that Your Father's business You had come to do.
According to the Father's plan, home with them You went,

Until the age of thirty, Your life with them was spent.
From twelve to thirty, wherever Your feet trod,
You grew in stature and favor, with man and with God.

You were baptized by the prophet John,
The dove descended and Your Father spoke:
This is My beloved Son in whom I am well pleased!

After forty days of fasting and temptation,
You started your ministry.
Rabbi—teacher—to teach Salvation's plan.
The incarnate Word of God, the Father's heart to man.
You healed the sick, lame, mute, and the blind,
Cast out demons, brought back the dead, and many other signs.

You came not to condemn but taught that man must be born again.
You fulfilled the law—fully God, fully man.
To reconcile us to the Father, You became the *passover lamb*.
You were born to die to pay the price that sin had placed on us.
You purchased our freedom with Your blood,
YOU the SINLESS, You the JUST!

In the Bible, I plainly read; satan tried to keep You from me.
To keep Your story from being told
so forever I would be in his hold.
You came to pay sins' debt for me. Your Blood
broke his chains and set me free.
Praise the Father, Son, and Holy Spirit,
You came for all men, if only they'd hear it.

This is what Christmas means to me; my heart wants to sing.
A new beginning, life without ending with You, my Lord and King.
Yeshua Hamashiach, in your Word You plainly say,
The only gift You want from me is the life I live each day.

I've learned to love Jewish customs and ways,
and I know You loved them too.
Sometimes I've wondered Lord, *What was Your favorite food?*
In all Your years upon this earth, before Your ministry, You
loved Your friends, Your Jewish heritage, and Your family.
You will always love Your people. You want us to love them too.
Most scriptures (if not all) from Genesis to
Revelation was written by a Jew.

In heaven, You are the Lion of Judah.
That will never change.
From Israel You ascended, it is there You'll return again.
In Revelation, You're Israel's Messiah,
Yes, our Savior too.
Glory, Honor, and Praise—all belong to You.
You are the Truth, the Life, and the Way.
Jesus Christ
Yeshua Hamashiach, Happy Birthday!

Forgive, Forgive, Forgive

(Based on Matthew 6:9–13)

When we hear the word *forgive*, it brings to mind a question. We know something is not right. Wrong has been done somehow, somewhere, someway. For each of us, it has been a reality we have had to face. Others have wronged us or we have wronged them.

Either way, forgiveness is a reality in life to be dealt with! Our world is filled with unforgiven and unforgiving people. They are broken and miserable. To live that way brings misery. People try so hard to fill that void with so many empty fillers. *Only Jesus Christ can fill it*! There are many reasons for our sins! God knows them all. Every hair on our head is numbered. He knows the intent of our thoughts. From the smallest to the worst, God is too Holy to excuse them. He did one better! He paid for them. He is full of mercy, love, and forgiveness! He gave that to us at the CROSS. We, then, are to give the same to others.

It costs *God* everything to forgive us. He gave us His only Son to die and pay for our sins. Jesus's BLOOD paid our sin's debt. Without that, we would all be condemned. He had declared and could not change that without the shedding of blood, there is no remission of sins. Hebrews 9:22 says it all! If He would do that for us who are sinful (although He was sinless), then it is *pride* in us, when we refuse to forgive others as though we are higher than God and *His Son*, and our pain is greater than Jesus suffered for us to be reconciled to the Father. The first thing God hates is *pride* (Proverbs 6:16–19). We must forgive! God understands how hard it is, and He will give you the strength to do so (Philippians 4:13). Just ask Him to (James 4:3).

Put Jesus first and see the CROSS. God knows the joy that will come in doing so. He wants us to walk in peace, and we will. If you don't, you will be eaten up with bitterness (Hebrews 12:15). *That bitterness is something unforgiving people feed on*! All wrong is caused by sin. Sin will maim, destroy, and kill, and cause horrible results. The only solution is forgiveness through *the Lord* and *His* strength (Philippians 4:13).

What He tells us is always for our good. God has made a way for us to be at peace and happy because of it. He knows better than anyone. He is the author of forgiveness. When someone violates His Word, *He calls it sin.* Someone gets hurt. The bigger the violation, the bigger the wound, the *deeper* the pain. We have to remember we live in a sin-cursed world. All Christians will have that to contend with. *Even at our best, we miss the mark (imperfection).* It can be a sin of commission or omission. Either way is a violation of God's Word (Romans 3:23). *God forgives us when we ask for it* (1 John 1:9)! *To forgive someone, we must look at our own life and remember when we (before Christ) sinned against God. Our own righteousness was as filthy rags* (Isaiah 64:6). *Jesus had to pay for all our sins, and He did that freely. Remember the cross and the cost. God forgave you! He also paid for the person's sins that wronged you. He loves them too.*

It's comparable to owing a debt to a mortgage company, and they sell the debt to another company. They do not have to ask you if they can do this. Like so when you forgive for Jesus's sake and turn the debt over to Jesus, and now He is in charge of it. That person owes Jesus. It is now between Jesus and the person that hurt you. You have nothing to do with it anymore. Jesus is your defense (Psalm 18:2). He will maintain your cause. *If, in your heart, you pray that person will get things right with God, you will get a measure of peace and happiness you would not expect and cannot explain. Just as Jesus forgave you, you really do forgive and are free.*

I feel like this. I would not want for any reason any person to miss heaven because of what they did to me on earth. I am not that important. That is for eternity. My God is so pleased when we obey Him in this. One thing I have learned, when we make Him happy, we get happy in ourselves. When we honor Him, He gives us honor. And we know that all things work together for good to them that love God, to them who are the called according to his purpose (Romans 8:28). That purpose is to glorify His Son. To forgive others as He has forgiven us!

Matthew 6:12–15, Can you read this and not forgive?

God's way is the answer for a peaceful life here on earth! Jesus came to give us life and life more abundant. Nothing goes unnoticed. He is a rewarder of those who diligently seek Him (Hebrews 11:6).

Ask for forgiveness and give it!

Acceptance

I was born November 8, 1937, in Gary, Indiana. Mine was kind of an untimely birth. My mother was ill from the onset of the pregnancy. She desired not to be pregnant and went on to reject me when I was born. This continued for several years, and others had to step in and care for me and my older sister. This may have been the reason a feeling of rejection seemed to be a part of my life for years. Like a cloud hanging over me, it was a mode I seemed to feel comfortable in. It would be hard to describe my growing up years. They were good, and they were bad. Normal in that respect. The era I grew up in was good in my mind, and still is to this day. I like anything concerning it, entertainment-wise. The music was far more romantic than it is now. Some have called me a hopeless romantic. I smile at that and wonder if it is true. Ah, but at least love had some substance to it and forever remained in the heart.

The music said this, and I like that.

As a young girl, I was really confused about many things. I had high aspirations but never lived up to them. In my mind, I just couldn't. I wanted to but felt I was a failure and, in the end, would be rejected. This was the case in so many things I did. Oh, I was told I was so pretty and had such a singing voice. Pumped up only to be deflated by reality checks. This caused hardships that shouldn't and wouldn't have been without the compliments heaped upon me (maybe overinflated in my mind, but who knows?).

Later in my life, I realized children should not be complimented on or given credit for things they could not take credit for. God alone is responsible for these things. Looks, talents, intelligence, etc. Compliments should be given on the things that they are responsible for, like character and behavior. These all have to do with choices. Choices are something they will have to make all their lives, and each one will determine their life and how it is spent. This can be done with encouragement and love and doesn't put undue pressure on them to succeed. They will want to, without comparing themselves to others, which sets them up for problems.

Healthy self-acceptance comes with this, in knowing that God designed each one of us to suit Him, we can live at peace with ourselves and others. However we look—be it color, features, or unchangeable things—we know it is His doing and no one else. He bears this responsibility, not us. We are only responsible for what we do with what He has made. When we truly understand this, we then choose not to poke fun at His handiwork, not ourselves or anyone else. We realize that He loves us because we are His special design. When we understand who He is and who we are because of Him, we can then get it right. Each child born needs to grow up with this teaching and understanding embedded into their consciousness. They will then enjoy the particulars, whatever they are.

Stressing that they are special, never to be on this earth again, sent for a purpose by the One who makes no mistakes, takes unneeded stress off them. When children are taught that each person has strengths and weaknesses, some wins and some failures, it helps them to be balanced. This is the reality of life. In accepting that life is difficult, it then becomes easier.

Little children grow up to be adults, and their childhood years are the foundation they build on all their adult years. In the physical world of construction, every foundation built needs and usually requires an inspection at each critical stage.

If it is faulty, sooner or later, there will be a collapse of some kind. The same holds true in a child's life. There are absolute principles to be adhered to. These principles are not grievous to apply, and they are structurally sound.

Absolutely!

Many argue that there are no absolutes. Tell that to a banker, a mechanic, a carpenter, a manufacturer, an astronaut, and a mathematician, etc. There is the right way or numerous wrong ways. The truth is always structured and can only be what it is. Wrong can be anything and as many ways as you want it to go. This applies to everything in life. Everything man has done, he has either done it right or it has been wrong. To build, there must be a plan with absolutes and absolutely upheld or it will, in time, prove the wrong that was done. And so it is with a life. There is a *plan*, there are *unchanging principles* to be followed. They will hold when all the elements come against it. It is a given that man did not make himself. Though he can (through the countless absolutes he has learned) and has made countless things, he will (if adhering to the absolute of *truth*) have to admit he did not make himself. And in his quest to find out how he is made (through many trials and errors) has on his part finally reached some understanding that the body he lives in follows many absolutes on its own accord.

It lives and runs in an absolute world of absolutes. If any variance happens, then man senses something is absolutely wrong and sees a doctor to see if he can make it return to the absolutes and function right again! This is an absolute truth. If then the body, which man lives in (which he did not make), follows absolutes on its own absolute, then it stands to reason that man should comply to the absolute of truth—that the world on the outside where he lives also has absolutes to follow. This is an absolute *truth*. Applying the principles of *truth* brings us to the absolutes of the *Ten Commandments*! Perfect Law.

Absolute: Only One ever lived perfectly.

The Son of God—Jesus—*absolutely perfect.*

Absolute: God's Word says in Romans 3:23, "All have sinned and come short of the Glory of God."

Absolute: God activated *salvation's plan* in John 3:16 that says, "For God so loved the world, that He gave His only begotten Son, that whosoever believeth in him should not perish, but have everlasting life."

Absolute: When you accept this and receive Jesus as your Lord and Savior, you are born again (in your spirit). You are forgiven and heaven bound.

Oh Happy Day!

Oh Happy Day

When I was growing up, I was filled with anger and bitterness. So many things weren't right, and I rebelled. I tried a lot of ways to show it.

This only made things worse. I couldn't see the root of my problems.

Then I had a life-changing experience. I was born again. Oh Happy Day! It was like someone had turned on a light. I began to see things differently and how different my life became.

It is like one who has worked hard on a puzzle and just can't find the connecting pieces to complete it. Then there they are! When my life was changed, the pieces needed were put into place. Though the final picture won't be completed until I leave this life, there is enough of it to show myself and others that the One who started it takes great joy in its completion. There is no better life, or may I say, there is no life without Him!

My Walk—Based on Psalm 138:8

Lord, I thank you for fifty-eight years
you've walked with me each day
Though there wasn't one of them I didn't fail you in some way
I often questioned how You could love someone like me
To cleanse me with Your Precious Blood, Lord how can it be?

I was just a babe in You, with much to learn and do
To be a follower was my desire, but could I follow through?
The Holy Spirit the Comforter, would lead me into Truth
To show me I was helpless, my strength would come from You

So many times I failed and on me I thought You'd quit
You forgave me and cleaned me up and that would just be it
You have taught me through the years, You want my whole heart
Then You will do the work in me, that's where it has to start

One day I read a verse, You will perfect that which concerns me
Psalm 138:8, what a promise, so happy I could be
My concerns were many, I began to list, prioritize them too
The Holy Spirit showed me, the first one
should be My Walk with You

I thank You Lord for this Truth of Truth,
My Walk, You will perfect it too

In Closing

If anyone, while reading this book has decided to be *born again*,

In other words,
If the Son of God your heart has won
sing and rejoice for the rest of your days
Obey His Word, give Him thanks and praise
All these things are what He is due
He made you He saved you and He'll see you through

Psalm 138:8 says it all,
pray it back to Him
let Him make your calls
address your concerns
but always begin
with number one being your walk with Him

John 3:7 says, "Marvel not that I said unto thee,
Ye must be born again" (Jesus's own words).

Martha Hernandez is eighty-five years young. She has been with her husband, Mike, for almost sixty-seven years. Together they have four children, Michael Jr., Daniel (Monica), Mimi (John), and Amber (Frank). They have seventeen grandchildren and forty-two great-grandchildren.

She has been blessed with lots of love, gifts of humor, laughter, and tears with her family, yet smiles shine through. God has given her a story to tell and a way to tell it (this book)! For this reason, it's Martha's desire to share her heart with you.